GREAT NATIONS AND LITTLE MINDS

AN ESSAY IN TODAY'S POLITICS

"A great empire and little minds go ill together"
– Edmund Burke 1775

Published by New Generation Publishing in 2025

Copyright © Peter Smith-Cullen 2025

First Edition

The author asserts the moral right under the Copyright, Designs and Patents Act 1988 to be identified as the author of this work.

All Rights reserved. No part of this publication may be reproduced, stored in a retrieval system or transmitted, in any form or by any means without the prior consent of the author, nor be otherwise circulated in any form of binding or cover other than that which it is published and without a similar condition being imposed on the subsequent purchaser.

ISBN: 978-1-83563-930-6

www.newgeneration-publishing.com

New Generation Publishing

Contents

Introduction v
Chapter 1 1
Chapter 2 15
Chapter 3 31
Chapter 4 43
Chapter 5 49
Chapter 6 53
Chapter 7 61

With many thanks to Geraldine for her diligent editing in making this little book possible

Introduction

The problem with history is determining the starting point as the cause to any event. Did the rise of Nazism and the Second World War begin with the Treaty of Versailles? Did the First World War begin with the assassination of an Archduke in Sarajevo? Did a divided Ireland start at the Battle of the Boyne or the UK leaving the EU rest with the politics of Boris Johnson? Do the current problems in Gaza originate with the decision by the United Nations in 1948 to create the State of Israel?

In each case a simple first response is to say yes, but of course the cause of each of those trigger events was long preceded by a history of earlier events.

So this leads to a question of the value of knowing and understanding history? Does anything happening in the world yesterday really contribute to a better understanding of events taking place today? And how much were those events affected by a key player? Was it the event that made history, or the person? Would history have changed with a different person?

So, is it better to understand the history and background to global events or the psychological makeup and motivations of that key individual? Of course, both are needed for a rounded view.

We learn so much more by understanding Donald Trump, Vladimir Putin, and Benjamin Netanyahu than just a knowledge of the history of the USA, Russia, or Israel.

Here we shall try to condense into a few brief chapters the key milestones that made each of these three countries what they are today. After each brief summary, we shall look at the background of three individuals, each now in their seventies and born within a few years of one another. We can decide why they consider now is the time to act in the national interest. Is that moment the result of an event that left them with no alternative, or is it an event that the individuals have long waited to exercise?

Summary of Chapters

Chapter 1

The USA beginning with its discovery by the West, its fight and establishment for Independence, the Great Depression, the New Deal, its support for Europe in two world wars, to today, when Donald Trump was elected for a second term.

Chapter 2

Brief History of Russia from Peter the Great. Marx and Engels. Lenin and the October Revolution, Stalin, Khrushchev and Cuba, Gorbachev and the Collapse of the USSR and the election of Putin.

A footnote on Zelensky and Ukraine.

Chapter 3

The Birth of Zionism and Theodore Hersl The Protecorate of Palestine and the Balfour Declaration, The Holocaust, the UN vote and the formation of the State of Israel, The Nakba, The 6-day war, and expansion of Israeli settlements. The election of Benjamin Netanyahu.

Chapter 4

Looks at the background of Donald Trump and his followers and questions why he feels the US has been taken massive advantage of by the rest of the world and that he alone was put here to "Make America Great Again".

Chapter 5

Looks at Vladimir Putin and his background from highly respected communist parentage to his role as a senior member of the KGB to today when he believes Russia has been ignored and exploited by a belligerent Western propaganda and military alliances to Russia's detriment and leaving him no alternative but to act.

Chapter 6

Explores the background of Benjamin Netanyahu, his military role in freeing hostages in Entebbe and his degrees from MIT and Harvard. He is probably the best educated of our three world leaders. We look at his trial for corruption and the reaction to the Hamas murders of 1,400 at an unguarded Kibbutz in the south of Israel. We question the deal he and Trump might be trying to establish for Palestine.

Chapter 7

Asks where each these individuals might be in five or six years' time, and a look into the future with a proposed ideal way out to each current predicament.

Chapter 1

A BRIEF HISTORY OF THE USA

English Colonists and the planting of Virginia

Legend has it in 1626 that Peter Minuit purchased Manhattan from the indigenous Native American tribe living there, the Lenape, for the equivalent in goods and money, of 60 guilders. He named the town New Amsterdam. Forty years later the British overcame the Dutch settlers and renamed it New York after the Duke of York.

At the same time settlers of much of Europe began to populate the Eastern Seaboard area. The southern area subsequently called Florida by the Spanish, Louisiana by the French, and Virginia and Cape Cod by the British.

In 1565, Spanish admiral Pedro Menedes de Aviles founded St Augustine in North Eastern Florida. It has been continuously inhabited since then, making it the oldest town in America.

Meanwhile, the French settlers specialised in fur trapping although the growing populations of towns like New Orleans necessitated more food production, and rice and meat became predominant. At this time, with the arrival of many slaves from West Africa, cotton harvesting was made easier and became an essential trading commodity.

The British settlers were mostly farmers, in the first instance to ensure an adequate supply of food for themselves. One such farmer from Norfolk, John Rolfe, discovered a hedgerow plant smoked by indigenous tribes, what we now know as tobacco. John Rolfe married a native American Princess, called Pocahontas, who had previously saved the life of John Smith, a fellow settler. Rolfe used his agricultural knowledge to cultivate tobacco on a grand scale, and it became a major trading commodity for the British.

Today almost 1 billion deaths are said to be from the direct result of smoking.

The British Empire and the Revolution

Between 1625 and (what the British call the War of Independence and the Americans call The Revolutionary War)in 1775, the colonial population had grown to over 2 million. To increase its revenues the British Government decided to impose more taxes on the colonists. This inevitably caused massive resentment. By 1773, there were growing calls for independence. No taxation without representation; the colonialists having had no say in the British Parliament over the imposition of such taxes. Colonists dressed up as Native Americans boarded a ship in Boston Harbour owned by the East India Company and jettisoned its entire cargo of tea into the harbour rather than pay the high price demanded. The British subsequently introduced the Intolerable Act designed to punish Massachusetts as an example to the other states rebelling in a similar way.

In 1775 Longfellow wrote a poem called *Paul Revere's Ride* in which Paul Revere shouts, "The British Are Coming," which has long since entered into American folk history as the start of the Revolutionary War. The United States of America declared its Independence from Britain on the 4 July 1776. George Washington had formed the Continental Army to fight against the retaliatory British and achieved a final decisive victory in 1781 against the British with the Siege of Yorktown; this battle in turn led George III in 1783 to concede the colonies to the Continental Army, ratified two years later with the treaty of Paris.

This treaty ensured the long-term future of the United States as an independent republic and set it on the road to become a future major global power.

The American Constitution

The American Constitution is arguably the oldest written constitution in the world and was brought into effect in 1789. It divides government power into 3 equal parts: The Legislature, The President, and The Judiciary, so that any two can effectively block a rogue third party. It also separates power between State and Federal Government.

1. The Legislature consisting of the Senate and the House of Representatives together called Congress.
2. The President himself and his officers.
3. The balancing act is the Judiciary, namely the Supreme and other Federal Courts.

The Constitution itself has been amended 27 times; the first 10 amendments constituting the Bill of Rights, including the freedom of speech and the right to bear arms, among others.

A further complication and need for urgent reform is the electoral college. Originally put in place to ensure States with smaller populations had a fair voice in the nominations of

President and Vice-President it is arguably no longer relevant. In 1969 the House voted for its abolition, as it is in most democracies with similar bodies, but it was voted down by the Senate. Opponents say it goes against the fundamental principle of one person, one vote.

The Growth of a New Democracy

The peaceful growth of the United States was largely at the expense of hundreds of thousands of Native Americans who were slaughtered and displaced and mass immigration from Britain, Ireland, Scandinavia, Poland, and other parts of Europe; some suggest over 50 million.

This otherwise peaceful growth was severely disrupted by 4 years of Civil War starting in 1861 triggered in the main by Abraham Lincoln's anticipated ban on slavery, principally in the Southern States. This in turn led to the formation of the Unionist army in the North fighting the Confederate Army in the South. Ultimately there was a Union victory in 1863, leading to the famous address by Lincoln in the immediate aftermath of the battle. In part, he said, *"... that we here highly resolve that these dead shall not have died in vain— that this nation, under God, shall have a new birth of freedom—and that government of the people, by the people, for the people, shall not perish from the earth."*

Woodrow Wilson, America First, and World War 1

Woodrow Wilson came to the Presidency in 1913 as 28th President. As a devout Christian he desperately wanted to keep America from intervening and interfering with foreign affairs, especially foreign wars and to concentrate on its domestic agenda. This America First ideology would be repeated in WW2, with Lindbergh and again in Donald Trump's "Make America Great Again".

Wilson's hope to keep America out of WW1 was thwarted by Germany engaging in submarine warfare despite previous assurances to the contrary, and in 1917 the United States entered the war. Woodrow Wilson continued after WW1 to play an active part in the promotion of peace with the formation of the League of Nations. This body was set up to resolve international disputes between nations peacefully and avoid conflict. Despite Wilson's extreme efforts the US refused to join the League.

Woodrow Wilson was nonetheless awarded the Nobel Peace Prize for his endeavours in 1919. He died in 1925.

The Expansion of Democracy

By 1920, women had gained the right to vote in the US. Despite almost doubling the democratic vote, it achieved no decisive advantage to either political party.

The Interwar Years

The ending of the First War began a period known as The Roaring Twenties. It was a great period of prosperity and consumerism on many fronts and brought about a multitude of dramatic social and technological changes.

Culturally, cinema and radio became known and loved by the general public, and Mickey Mouse was born. Writers such as Earnest Hemingway, F Scott Fitzgerald and later, Gertrude Stein and John Steinbeck joined the host of American authors to create of surge of new literature. Film stars such as Clark Gable and Errol Flynn with their celebrity status and fantastic homes in Hollywood, promoted a celebrity lifestyle previously unknown. Americans lapped up gossip and fan magazines and the Cult of Celebrity was born.

In New Orleans a new musical genre called Jazz appeared and musicians such as Count Basie, Duke Ellington, and Louis Armstrong were heard in the clubs and on the radio throughout the country. Jazz also found a natural home in the Speakeasy clubs, during prohibition (between 1920 and 1933) where alcohol was illegally sold. Prohibition was finally abandoned after the Government realised it was losing millions in potential tax revenues and to eliminate the black market for alcohol.

Automobile ownership soared from 6% in 1929 to more than 40% by 1940. Consumerism started to be aimed at women, with the introduction of home electrical goods such as refrigerators, washing machines, vacuum cleaners, toasters, and kettles… all of which could be bought and paid for by in-store credit.

All good things came to an end in October 1929 when the stock market on Wall Street crashed. The result was 40% of US banks going out of business; there having been very little regulation to safeguard assets at that time. An important related consequence in history was that Germany who had been heavily dependent on US banks, suffered dire financial losses leading ultimately to the election of Adolf Hitler.

Unemployment reached one in four of the working population and a third of farmers lost their land.

In 1930 the Hoover Government tried to avert the crisis by imposing high tariffs on imported goods. These tariffs only had the effect of exacerbating the effects of the depression, with most economists today describing them as catastrophic. Initially, Donald Trump's attempts to impose crippling tariffs in his second term caused wide spread financial panic and he was forced to reconsider.

In 1933, Franklin D Roosevelt became the 32nd President of the United States. His first 100 days in office saw the introduction of The New Deal and the three Rs: Relief, Recovery, and Reform. Anticipating criticism, he announced: "The only thing to fear is fear itself." Relief to provide essential financial support to the unemployed, Recovery by investing heavily in infrastructure programs to provide employment, and lastly, Reform of the Stock Market and Banking sector. In July, Roosevelt addressed the nation on the radio to record his success and achievements during his first 100 days in office, a practice that others carry out to this day. Although quick to act he was equally quick to change direction when he got things wrong.

The depression was to end by the close of the decade in part brought about by the advent of WW2. .

World War 2

Following on from WW1, the America First ideology was kept alive by Charles Lindbergh, an aviator who came to fame as the first person to fly across the Atlantic from New York to Paris in his single engine plane, The Spirit of St Louis in 1927. Like President Wilson before him, he was a strong and popular advocate for keeping America out of WW2.

But circumstances conspired, and again, America was dragged into the War by the invasion of Pearl Harbour, in Hawaii, by the Japanese in December 1941.

Within 6 months, the US secured a major victory in the Pacific against Japan with the Battle of Midway and sank 4 Japanese aircraft carriers.

America played a significant role in the defeat of Nazi Germany and was the largest manufacturer of armaments, aircraft, tanks, guns, and ships in the world.

On the 6 June 1944, Allied Forces began the joint invasion of 5 beaches in Normandy on the northern French coast. Dwight D Eisenhower was appointed Supreme Commander of the Allied Forces. From the initial landings until the end of the War, almost 1 million troops were in Europe and progressively liberated countries from German occupation as well as the complete destruction and surrender of Germany. Adolf Hitler took his own life in a bunker in Berlin on 30 April 1945.

Germany officially surrendered at Reims, France on 7 May 1945, which ended the war in Europe. The war in Japan ended in September after America dropped that atom bomb.

As an allied victory looked likely, The Yalta Conference was convened in February 1945 in Crimea, USSR, with President Roosevelt, Joseph Stalin, and Winston Churchill to decide what to do with Germany at the conclusion of the

War. Ultimately, Germany was split into zones, as was Berlin and each of the 3 leaders would have their own zones of interest.

The atom bomb dropped on Japan was developed in Los Alamos, New Mexico, where in 1943, a group of the world's leading scientists including Enrico Fermi and Albert Einstein had gathered to harness nuclear energy into a bomb under the supervision of Robert Oppenheimer, in what was to be known as The Manhattan Project.

Although it succeeded in its warlike intention, nuclear power went in the next few decades to become the major source of energy away from the use of fossil fuels.

Arguably, the Two World Wars represented the biggest challenge of the twentieth century and the United States of America had proved itself to be not only a Great Nation but perhaps the Greatest Nation. Similarly, Franklin D. Roosevelt was undoubtedly a mind of considerable intellect and fortitude.

The Cold War

Immediately after the War in 1945, the United Nations was formed with the objective to ensure world peace through dialogue. From the initial 51 nations, it has today 193 members; 5 members have a special status: Russia, United

States, China, France, and the United Kingdom, and any one can effectively block any resolution proposed and agreed by its members.

NATO is a military organisation headquartered in Brussels and was set up in 1949 to combat any threat by the Soviet Union. Long after the dissolution of the Soviet Union, NATO has continued to grow and considered by the Russian Federation to be an offensive rather than a defensive body.

The aftermath of WW2 saw the growth of a new world order. Whereas the Soviet Union was once an ally of the US, now the US regarded it their major enemy with its communist ideology. The Cold War began with the US and the Soviet Union vying for supremacy.

In the Far East, America was determined to stop the spread of communism. The Korean War began in 1950 with the US fighting against communist North Korea. It lasted 3 years with no clear victor; North Korea remains communist and South Korea is a Western friendly republic separated by the 38th parallel and a well-defended Demilitarized Zone.

In 1955, America took over from the French in fighting the communist Vietcong in Vietnam. Lynden B Johnson led America into the Vietnam War to avert the so-called domino effect of communist influence and ideology in South East Asia after Korea. It was to last 20 years before it ended in humiliating defeat for America in 1975, having lost thousands of young men. The use of Agent Orange, a defoliant and Napalm, an accelerant, by the US caused horrifying injuries and ongoing genetic abnormalities in the local population and is considered by many to be a war crime. Vietnam is now the Socialist Republic of Vietnam – communist.

The Suez crisis of 1956 demonstrated the impotence of the old European powers when France and Britain tried unsuccessfully to retake the Suez Canal from Egyptian control by force with Israeli support; condemned by the UN and the United States. The British had earlier reneged on a promise to fund the building of the Aswan Dam, leading to President Nasser's decision to nationalise the Canal. This strengthened the concept of a world order of two superpowers.

The Cold War came to an end with the breakup of the Soviet Union, the reunification of Germany, and the demolition of the Berlin Wall in 1989.

In the twenty-first century, America has, like the rest of world, grappled with economic inequality, social unrest, and political polarization.

In 2009, Barack Obama was elected as the first Black President.

Donald Trump, the first President to have no political background whatsoever, became President in 2016, stood again and lost to Joe Biden in 2020, attempted to overturn that election, and rallied his supporters to storm the Capitol Building in 2021. He's now serving a second term.

Chapter 2

A BRIEF HISTORY OF RUSSIA

Peter the Great and Russia Before 1917

Peter 1, known as Peter the Great, was born in 1672. He was to become Tsar of all Russia, but only being a child, he ruled jointly with his half-brother between 1682 and 1689. He became Emperor of All Russia in 1712.

When he was 16, he discovered an interest in boats and taught himself how to sail. He studied arithmetic, geometry, and military sciences, and by 1694 Peter set an imposing figure, standing over 2 metres tall. He became known for his reforms and projects to modernise and Westernise Russia. He travelled extensively, particularly to the Netherlands and Britain where he studied 'modern things' like ship building and warfare. He won military victories over Russia's great historic rivals, the Ottoman Empire and the Kingdom of Sweden, thus able to make territorial gains and set up the Russian Navy.

Peter founded St Petersburg in 1703 on the site of a captured Swedish fortress. For Russians, St Petersburg is historically and culturally associated with the birth of the Russian Empire and Russia's entry in to modern history as a European great power. Peter moved the capital from Moscow to St Petersburg in 1712, where it stayed until 1918.

In 1728, Vitus Bearing, a Russian of Danish origins, explored the 80-km wide strait between Asian Russia and the Americas and named it the Bearing Straight. The Russian Empire was the first to colonise this area, calling it Russian America. However, it being the most North Easterly point of the Empire, and costly to maintain, it was sold to the USA in 1867 for $7.2 million, becoming Alaska, one of the two non contiguous US States.

Peter the Great died aged 52 in 1725.

Karl Marx and Frederick Engels

Karl Marx and Frederick Engels were both Prussian; Karl was born in 1818 and Frederick two years later in 1820. They were to meet in Paris in 1844, and Engels became Marx's lifelong friend, collaborator, and major benefactor; constantly bailing Marx out after his frequent spells of profligacy and poverty.

Engels had established his socialist credentials with the publication of The Condition of the Working Class in England in 1845 after living for a period in Manchester.

In 1849, Marx, with support from Engels, wrote and published the Communist Manifesto printed originally in Germany, and then, in 1850 translated into English. The cornerstone of the Communist Manifesto included the introduction of a progressive income tax, the nationalisation of banks, communications and transportation, the gradual abolition of inherited wealth and land, the abolition of child labour, and education to be freely available to all.

After expulsion from his homeland, Marx eventually settled in the UK in 1849, where he was to spend the rest of his life. Much of his time was spent in Dean Street in London; his house bears a blue plaque to this day and was walking distance from the British library, where he was to write his greatest work.

Expanding on a favourite theme; the exploitation of the proletariat by the holders of capital, resulted in the publication of the first volume of Das Kapital in 1867. It would ultimately run to 3 volumes and published in many languages; the last two posthumously.

It is easy to dismiss this work in the light of the wealth of the middle and working classes in the Western world today but in 1820, the average income of the top 10% was 18 times higher than lowest 50%; in 2020 the average income of the top 10% was 38 times higher than the lowest 50% (as quoted from the World Inequality Report published in 2022).

Engels was only one of a few attendees at Marx's funeral in March 1883, along with his daughter Eleanor. He was buried alongside his wife who had died of cancer just over a year before, in Highgate Cemetry in London. Engels died 12 years later in London from throat cancer and had his ashes scattered from Beachy Head in Sussex.

Marx and Engels could well be considered the fathers of Communism and as such have been loved and loathed in equal measure throughout the world.

Lenin, Trotsky, and The October Revolutions

March 1917 should have seen the start of a New World Order for Russia, with the abdication of the last Romanov Tsar, Nicholas II. The First World War had brought havoc to Russia who was not only doing badly on the battlefield, but massive food shortages were combined with a perceived lack of political leadership.

A train west of Petrograd (St Petersburg renamed after 1914) carrying Nicholas and his family, was stopped by revolutionaries and held for a number of days. It was here Nicholas signed away his future and abdicated. Although a half-hearted attempt was made to relocate them to England; George V and Nicolas were cousins, this was eventually rejected because of worries of political unrest spreading to the UK.

In October, a provisional government in Petrograd was overthrown by Vladimir Lenin, Head of the Bolshevik party and Leon Trotsky, Head of the Red Army. The Bolsheviks established their own government and proclaimed the establishment of the Russian Soviet Federative Socialist Republic, which ultimately became the USSR, and moved the capital back to Moscow.

Nicolas, his wife Alexandra, and their 5 children, were imprisoned at the Ipatiev house in Yekaterinburg, and in 1918, they were shot by the Bolsheviks and buried in a nearby forest.

Joseph Stalin and Lavrentiy Beria

Stalin was born on December 1878 in a small wooden house, preserved today as a museum. He trained for the Russian Orthodox priesthood but eventually dropped out.

He was enthralled by Lenin and the other Bolshevik revolutionaries and even resorted to crime to fund the new party and became editor of the Pravda newspaper.

Stalin was made a member of the Politburo and in 1922 became Secretary General and gained control over the party bureaucracy. After Lenin died in 1924, he won Party leadership over rival Leon Trotsky.

He was to become a deadly and formidable dictator in what became known as Stalinism; never trust anyone who has an ism at the end of their name.

With Lavrentiy Beria, his trusted head of the NKVD (Secret Police), Stalin sent literally millions of Soviet citizens to work and die in the gulags and mines of Siberia. Luckily for the West, though, in June 1942, Nazi Germany embarked on a road to defeat by attacking Russia with Operation Barbarossa. Russia became an ally against Hitler. Despite eventual victory, Russia suffered the most casualties of WW2, estimated in excess of 26 million dead.

By the end of 1944, the outcome of the War was apparent, and the three Western leaders, Roosevelt, Stalin, and

Churchill, met in Yalta on the Crimean Peninsula. The objective was to agree the occupation of Germany after the War, effectively dividing the country, and Berlin; the East to the Russians, the North to the British, and the South to the Americans.

After the War, in 1945, Beria was instructed to build Russia's first nuclear bomb; this he did in Kazakhstan in August 1949, so now both super powers had the bomb.

Stalin died of a stroke in March 1953 and shortly after Nikita Khrushchev staged a coup d'etat and had Beria executed.

Khrushchev, Sputnik, Suez, and Cuba

Nikita Khrushchev was born in 1894. He was twice on the cover of Time Magazine; firstly, in 1953 when he became Secretary General and then in 1957 as *Man of the Year* following the successful launch of Sputnik 1. This satellite was a mere 2 feet in diameter with 4 protruding aerials but was capable of sending radio signals all over the world.

His first real position was in 1938 when he was sent to Ukraine as Head of the Communist Party.

He organised local elections, and formed the Ukrainian Soviet Socialist Republic based in Kiev. However, by 1941 with the War in progress, the Germans succeeded in capturing most of Ukraine and Khrushchev was sent to Stalingrad. As the War closed, Khrushchev was sent back to Ukraine to take part in its rebuilding; the country had been devastated and most of Kiev lay in ruins.

After Stalin's death and the execution of Beria, Khrushchev became the First Secretary of The Communist Party. One of his first acts was to transfer Crimea from Russian to Ukrainian control, largely because of his experience and fondness for the country.

But more notable was his 'Secret Speech' which he delivered in 1954. In it, he roundly denounced Stalin and all his actions. As a result, over the coming year, thousands of political prisoners were freed from gulags across Siberia.

1956 saw trouble in the Middle East with the final recognition by the old Imperial powers of France and Britain of their declining influence. Egyptian President Gamal Nasser wanted to ensure his country had control of the Suez Canal. In November 1956, British and French Forces, backed by Israel, attacked Egypt to regain control. This action was immediately condemned by the United Nations, Russia, and the United States, and led to the humiliating withdrawal of all invasion forces including Israel's presence in the Gaza Strip. For the next twenty years Russia was able to strongly influence and support Egypt both economically and militarily, especially with the construction of the Aswan Dam.

In 1958, attention returned to the German question and Berlin in particular. Since the end of the War Germany had been in effect two states, East and West, with access to Berlin through a corridor through East Germany. Russia asked the other occupying powers to effectively recognise two separate states; this they refused to do. That status quo remained until the collapse of the Berlin Wall nearly 40 years later.

In 1959 Khrushchev went to the United States at the invitation of Vice-President Nixon which included a meeting with President Eisenhower at Camp David.

In 1960, an American high altitude spy plane, known as the U2, was shot down over Soviet airspace. Its pilot, Gary Powers, was captured alive, tried by the Soviets for treason and imprisoned for 10 years. Khrushchev demanded an apology and a complete cessation of all flights over Russian territory without prior permission. No apology was forthcoming causing a major crisis in US/Soviet relations, leading to the collapse of the Paris Summit, where the UK, US, USSR, and France were to discuss disarmament

In the 1960s, Cuba and Russia became alarmed by what it saw as American aggression. The US were placing Jupiter nuclear missiles in both Turkey and Italy and at the same time the CIA organised a group of Cuban expatriates to invade Cuba in what was to be known as *The Bay of Pigs* fiasco. Fidel Castro repelled the invasion but was unsettled enough to seek assistance from the Soviet Union. Although initially reluctant, the Soviet Union agreed in 1962 to send a shipment of nuclear missiles to be based in Cuba, to avoid future aggression. However, somewhere over the Atlantic the now infamous spy planes spotted the shipment, leading to an historic announcement by John F Kennedy aimed at the Soviet Union. He announced an immediate naval blockade of Cuba. However, subject to the verifiable removal of all missiles from Cuba, the US would undertake never again to mount an invasion. The Russian ships turned around and a potential nuclear war was averted.

In April 1961 Russia achieved it first manned space flight when Yuri Gagarin successfully circumnavigated the earth. Thus, the Space War/Race was to join the Cold War. This Russian success led John F Kennedy to promise a month later that America would have a man on the moon by the end of the sixties. America just managed to achieve this in 1969.

Khrushchev retired two years later and spent the last eight of so years of his life at his Dacha in the country, before his death in 1971, aged 77.

Mikhail Gorbachev

Mikhail Gorbachev was born in Southern Russia in 1931 into poverty, like most Russian leaders. His mother was Ukrainian and he was was brought up in the Russian Orthodox Church, although later in life he professed to being an Atheist.

He became widely familiar in the West, not only because of the port-coloured birthmark on his forehead, but his substantial and widespread reforms, which led to the break-up of the Soviet Union, and influence on world politics. He was also the recipient of the Nobel Peace Prize.

After graduating from the Moscow University in 1955, he became engaged in politics and by 1985 was elected Secretary General of the Communist Party. One of his first acts was to end the Soviet occupation of Afghanistan. From mid-1988 saw the complete removal of Soviet troops; however, internal fighting in the country was to continue for many years until the final retreat of American troops and government by the Taliban in 2021.

Significantly, in October 1986, President Reagan and Gorbachev met in Reykjavik, Iceland, and agreed mutually to a substantial reduction of the deployment of long-range nuclear missiles and to put an end to the Cold War.

Gorbachev was now free to pursue two of his great goals: Glasnost and Perestroika. The first, Glasnost, was to permit and encourage free speech but in reality, whistleblowers, to point out deficiencies in the state apparatus. Perestroika was about both economic and political domestic reforms to reduce layers of bureaucracy from decision making.

The Unification of East and West Germany was achieved in November 1990 with the Berlin Wall being progressively dismantled thereafter. Sources say that George Baker, the US Secretary of State, had confirmed to Gorbachev that NATO would not be part of German defence although no such written confirmation of this has ever been found.

Of significance was Gorbachev's shared condemnation, with President George W. Bush, of Iraq's invasion of Kuwait in August 1990 and demanded their withdrawal. He did not condone, however, the subsequent invasion of Iraq by American troops in 1991 and its attack on Baghdad with its policy of Shock and Awe, and ultimate overthrow and execution of Saddam Hussain.

In October 1990 Gorbachev was awarded the Nobel Peace Prize for ending the Cold War, the planned unification of Germany and introducing the freedom of independence to the Soviet satellite countries.

Whilst on a brief holiday in Crimea, in August 1991, Gorbachev was detained by a group of Hardliners. After a few days Boris Yeltsin, in a tank on the Moscow White House lawn, demanded Gorbachev's release. Gorbachev returned to Moscow and promptly resigned passing the baton to Yeltsin. This in turn was passed to Vladimir Putin in May 2000.

Gorbachev retired with a string of lucrative television and journalism assignments, especially in the US and had a couple of unsuccessful forays back to political life. His wife, Raisa died of cancer after treatment in Germany in 1999 and Gorbachev died in August 2022 aged 91.

Vladimir Putin succeeded him and annexed Crimea in 2014 and invaded Ukraine in 2022; that war is ongoing.

Donald Trump said he'd end the war in a week when he took office in January 2025, hoping for a Nobel Peace Prize

A Footnote on Volodymyr Zelensky and Ukraine

Volodymyr Zelensky is the youngest leader in this essay. He was born in January 1978 in central Ukraine as a native Russian speaker. His great grandfather and other members of the family were killed in the Holocaust. He won a grant to study in Israel, but his father wanted him to remain in Ukraine, so he studied law in Kiev, but never actually practiced.

At 17, and still at university, he ventured into drama and comedy. Each year, he would enter the KVN Comedy Competitions and in 1995, his team won. He formed his own comedy group, Kvartal 95, that moved to the Ukrainian TV Channel, Inter in 2005.

He acted in several major films between 2015 and 2018 and was the voice of Paddington Bear for Ukrainian children. Interestingly, he played the role of a Ukrainian President in a Russian TV series called *A Servant to the People*.

After initially denying his intention to enter politics, he subsequently did so, and in April 2019, he was elected

President of Ukraine, promising his government would serve with honesty and integrity from day 1.

In October 2021, the so-called Pandora Papers published a major expose of secret funds held in bank accounts in Belize, the British Virgin Islands and Cyprus by Zelensky and his inner circle. Much of the money was invested in the London property market.

Documents show that just before he was elected, he gifted his stake in a key offshore company in the BVI to his business partner, soon to be his top presidential aide. The documents also show that an arrangement was made that would allow the offshore to keep paying dividends to a company that now belongs to his wife.

Politically, in his early years in office, Zelensky certainly tried to bring a certain rapprochement between Ukraine and Russia, until the Russian invasion in 2022.

Chapter 3

The Birth of Zionism, Israel and 125 years of fighting

Theodore Herzl and the birth of Zionism

Just before the end of the nineteenth century a young lawyer and journalist began a movement that would change forever the peace and tranquillity of the peoples of the Middle East. That man was Theodore Herzl. He was born in Pest in Hungary in 1860 and formed a Zionist movement to establish a homeland in Palestine for diasporic Jews. His ideas were firmly rejected by both the German emperor and the head of the Ottoman Empire, who controlled Palestine at that time. He even attempted for a short while to set up a temporary refuge in Uganda with support from Britain's Joseph Chamberlain, but all these attempts failed. He died of a heart attack at the age of 44, but today he is considered the spiritual head of Israel.

The Balfour Declaration

This was just a letter written in 1917 by Arthur Balfour, then British Foreign Secretary, to his friend Lord Rothschild, leader of the British Jewish community, as an expression of sympathy to the concept of a homeland for Jewish People in then Ottoman controlled Palestine. The Ottomans had ruled over a huge swath of the Middle East and North Africa for over 600 years with tolerance and fairness to multiple faiths, albeit mostly Islamic, and ethnicities.

The letter read::

Dear Lord Rothschild,

I have much pleasure in conveying to you, on behalf of His Majesty's Government, the following declaration of sympathy with Jewish Zionist aspirations which has been submitted to, and approved by the Cabinet.

His Majesty's Government view with favour the establishment in Palestine of a national home for the Jewish people, and will use their best endeavours to facilitate the achievement of this object, **it being clearly understood that nothing shall be done which may prejudice the civil and religious rights of existing non-Jewish communities in**

Palestine, or the rights and political status enjoyed by Jews in any other country.

Clearly the highlighted section of the letter was ignored.

Palestine Between the World Wars

After the end of the WW1 and the fall of the Ottoman Empire, Britain successfully secured a mandate for Palestine in 1922 which incorporated the sentiment of the Balfour Declaration. Jewish influence continued to grow including the creation of the Hebrew University of Jerusalem with the full support of Albert Einstein and Sigmund Freud. During this period the Jewish population in the area was greatly enlarged, as was the creation of Haganah, a Zionist military organisation established to defend and support the ideals and objectives of their movement.

World War 2 and The Holocaust

Before WW2 there were an estimated 10 million Jews living in every part of the US, Continental Europe, and the UK. Germany had suffered greatly as the result of pronouncements of the Treaty of Versailles in 1922 after WW1 and in the 1930s, Adolf Hitler increasingly used the Jewish population as a scapegoat for his nation's woes and began to place ever more restrictions on them. There were an estimated 500,000 Jews living in Germany at the time representing a very small proportion of the population of Germany as a whole. Nonetheless, they were blamed for the high interest rates charged by banks and money lenders, resulting in business failures generally. During this period many Jews were encouraged to emigrate and many in fact did so, albeit to countries in Europe where the Nazi influence would catch up with them.

In 1941, Hitler continued his anti-Semitic drive, initially forcing all Jews to wear a Yellow Star and appointing Reinhard Heydrich as head of a programme of extermination. Between 1941 and 1945, Nazi Germany and its allies systematically murdered 6 million Jews across German occupied Europe, mostly in concentration camps in Poland.

The Stern Gang, Haganah and Irgun: Terrorists or Fighters for a Just Cause

The Stern Gang, otherwise known by their preferred name of Lehi was founded in 1940 by Avraham Stern, to fight the British occupation despite the ongoing events of WW2 and to establish a Jewish homeland in Palestine. They even sought, unsuccessfully, an alliance with Germany believing the Nazis to be more sympathetic to their cause than Britain.

In November 1944, The British Minister for the Middle East, Walter Edward Guinness, Lord Moyne, (of the famous Irish Brewing family) was shot and killed by Lehi. The two assailants were subsequently caught and hanged.

In 1946, The Irgun, another Anti-British Zionist militia and militant movement blew up the King David Hotel in Jerusalem, which was serving as offices for the British Mandatory Authorities, killing over 91 people, most of them British, ostensibly to destroy documents.

The question of terrorist or freedom fighter depends on your perspective. The Stern Gang and Irgun were Zionist terrorists from the perspective of the British at the time, due to acts of violence and killing outside the parameters of a war. They, however, regarded themselves as fighting for a just cause, the creation of a Jewish homeland.

The United Nations Vote and the Creation of The State of Israel

Britain had been responsible for the management and protection of Palestine since 1922. After WW2 and the Holocaust and the growing call for the partitioning of Palestine to create a Jewish homeland, Britain referred the matter to the United Nations for a resolution.

In November 1947 the UN General Assembly voted for a partition plan; Resolution 181, which proposed both a Jewish and an Arab state in former British Mandated Palestine, to take place when the British mandate expired 6 months later. Most voted in favour, including the US and the Soviet Union and of the opposing votes, most came from Arab states. There were ten abstentions, one of which was Great Britain, who was concerned about the implementation and policing of the partition without further loss of life; fears which turned out to be well founded. .

The Nakba

Nakba in Arabic means Catastrophe. The formal recognition by the UN of a Jewish homeland in 1948 alongside an Arab state, and the departure of the British led to a major offensive by Israeli forces to remove Palestinians from adjoining villages and countryside. This resulted in the displacement of approximately half of the Palestinians living there. Six months later the United Nations called upon Israel to cease the war and allow the Arab refugees to return and resettle in their homes; UN Resolution 194. This was ignored by Israel.

The United Nations Relief and Works Agency (UNRWA) for Palestine Refugees in the Near East, was created by the United Nations General Assembly in December 1949, to provide direct relief and works programmes for Palestinian refugees following the 1948 Arab-Israeli conflict. The agency's mandate includes education, healthcare, relief, social services, protection, and emergency assistance and was up and running by May 1950. They operate in the West Bank, including East Jerusalem, Gaza, Jordan Lebanon and Syria.

UNRWA defines a Palestine refugee as someone whose normal place of residence was in Palestine between June 1946 and May 1948, and who lost both their home and means of livelihood due to the 1948 conflict. Descendants of male refugees are also considered refugees.

UNRWA is funded almost entirely by voluntary contributions. Historically, most of the agency's funds came from the United States and the European Commission; in 2019, close to 60% of its pledge of $1 billion came from EU countries, with Germany being the largest donor. In 2005, Israel pulled out of its occupation of Gaza but built a boundary wall.

Many Palestinians in the West Bank are refugees living under the longest occupation in history, and the rest face constant violent encounters with militant illegal Israeli settlers. At the end of 2024, Israel banned UNRWA from Gaza on the grounds it had been infiltrated by Hamas terrorists. So far, no evidence has been provided to substantially support the claim.

The 6-Day War

The so-called 6-day war in June 1967 was in fact just the largest of 3 wars or skirmishes that took place after signing the Armistice Agreements in 1949.

Nasser, President of Egypt had attempted to close the 8-mile gulf between the Sinai and the Arabian peninsulas at the Red Sea and the Gulf of Aqaba. This blockage would have lost Israel access to Eilat its Southern most port.

This prompted Israel to take the most drastic counter measures to date. Israel continues to claim it was a pre-emptive strike against Egypt, Syria, and Jordan, and only done to prevent an offensive operation. However, the net result was disaster for the Arabs with Israel claiming massive new territory. It took control of the Gaza Strip and the Sinai Peninsula from Egypt, the Golan Heights from Syria, and The West Bank and East Jerusalem from Jordan. Almost 500,000 Palestinians and Syrians were exiled from their lands in the aftermath of the war.

Nasser subsequently resigned but Egypt kept the Suez Canal closed until 1975.

The Oslo Accord

In September 1993, following a series of secret meetings in Oslo, President Bill Clinton invited both Yasser Arafat (the P.L.O. Chairman) and Yitzak Rabin (the Israeli Prime Minister) to the White House to sign the Accord. It was the first time these warring individuals had ever met. The agreement was considered temporary for 5 years until replaced by a permanent one, ensuring the rights and safety of both peoples. In the agreement the IDF would withdraw its troops from large parts of Gaza and the West Bank and be the authority responsible for their management.

Watching this potentially highly significant event was Benjamin Netanyahu. He was sickened and repulsed by this rapprochement of the PLO. Sixteen years earlier, Netanyahu had fought alongside his elder brother, as members of Israel's elite commando forces in Entebbe, after the hijack by the PLO of an Air France plane that was forced to land there. All the hostages were released but there was one Israeli fatality – Neyanyahu's brother Yonatan.

The fate of the two main signatories ensured the sad irrelevance of the well-intended Oslo Accords. Within 2 years Yitzhak Rabin was assassinated by a fellow Israeli opposed to the agreement and Yasser Arafat died in 2004 without explanation having been confined in his house in

Ramallah by the Israelis for over two years. The Nobel prizes awarded to them for their attempted peace effort are now gathering as the asymmetrical war continues.

The current Prime Minister is Benjamin Netanyahu, who was last elected in 2022.

The 7 October 2023 Attack by Hamas and Israel's Retaliation

On the 7 October, Hamas militants crossed the border into Israel from Gaza, murdered 1,200 Israeli citizens and took 280 hostages back into Gaza. The IDF retaliated with force, initially laying Gaza under siege, and cutting off all aid into the Strip. Almost immediately Israel began extensive bombing of Gaza; their stated aim being to destroy Hamas and get all the hostages freed.

What started off as justified self-defence, has long since become revenge and Gaza has been raised to the ground with the 2 million civilian population moved up and down the strip to reach aid, find shelter, and try to avoid falling munitions.

A ceasefire was negotiated at the end of 2024 that was to be in 3 phases. Hostages started to be released in exchange for Palestinian prisoners in Israel, aid started flowing back into Gaza after being severely curtailed by Israel, and

Palestinians started returning to their homes – what was left of them. But in March 2025, when the second phase was about to start, Israel reneged and broke the ceasefire, bombs started falling again, and there was again a total blockade of aid.

Donald Trump had vowed to rid Gaza of all 2 million Palestinians by forcing both Jordan and Egypt to accept them in return for continued US financial aid. The Gaza Strip itself would be rebuilt by Trump to become the Riviera of the Middle East. Trump's ludicrous proposition emboldened Israel to break the ceasefire and as of writing, famine is looming and Palestinians in Gaza are in a hopeless situation.

In Israel, Netanyahu is facing questions about the security failure that led to the attack. Some say that it wasn't a failure at all; that he gave Hamas the opportunity to breach the border intentionally, as an excuse to wipe Gaza off the map once and for all.

Sadly, the West has allowed this massacre to unfold. Netanyahu has made it clear that any criticism of his actions, or the actions of the Israeli government are anti-Semitic, so there has been reluctance to comment, although, in May 2025 a joint message of condemnation was sent from France, UK, and Canada, for Israel to stop the Gaza offensive.

There remain about 60 hostages in Gaza, of whom half are believed to be alive.

Chapter 4

Little Minds

Donald Trump

Donald Trump was born in 1946. His father, Fred was very cold and domineering. His children hardly dared speak to him for fear of reprimand. His mother, Mary Anne, was fragile and neglected the children, and so they constantly sought their father's approval. Trump today yearns for respect and peer recognition more than anything else. But where Vladimir Putin, for example, yearns for respect for Russia, his country, Donald Trump yearns only for respect for himself.

His father assumed that his older brother, Fred Junior, would take over the property business and therefore devoted his grooming and bullying to Fred Jr. Fred could only take so much and left to take up flying, joining TWA as a commercial pilot. Constantly belittled by his father and his brother, he eventually took to drink, was fired by TWA, and after several failed attempts to get back into his father's good books, died a few years later at 42 of a heart attack.

To get his way, Trump had become a natural bully; he will always pick on those he perceives as weaker than him, which, whether as President or not, he sees as most everyone else. He learnt to be a bully at The New York Military Academy where his parents hoped he'd learn discipline. He considered only those boys stronger than him to be worthy of his respect.

He was exempted for medical reasons from the draft and thus avoided Vietnam; the only uniform he ever wore was from his Military Academy. He went from there via Fordham University to Wharton College at the University of Pennsylvania and graduated in 1968 with a degree in Economics.

Trump joined his father Fred in the building and property business. Trump Snr became very rich, exploiting connections with the Democratic Mayor and while Donald played an active role in expanding the business, it was without, in later years being able to play on Fred's previous connections. He became the president of the family's real estate business in 1971, renamed it the Trump Organisation and began acquiring and building skyscrapers, among them Trump Tower and Trump Plaza in Manhattan, golf courses, and casinos. In 2004, he launched the reality TV show, *The Apprentice*, which served to reinforce his billionaire persona. He soon ran into financial difficulties, however, and was only saved by filing for several bankruptcies which allowed him to restructure the debt.

Trump manifested a passing interest in politics during the 1980s working to promote a Vietnam veterans memorial and in the presidential Fitness and Sport awards. He also spoke on a number of occasions to the Conservative Political Action Conference (CPAC). When Barack Obama came to power in 2009, Trump became highly vocal in claiming Obama was not born in the USA and thus not entitled to be its President. This claim was unfounded as he was in fact born in Hawaii. Nonetheless, it gave Trump the confidence and exposure to win the Republican vote in the upcoming Presidential election. He duly won the election in 2016 despite losing the popular vote to Hilary Clinton.

He is the only president to have had no previous political career. The fact that he was never a State Governor, or a Senator or a Congressman, did not detract from the appeal to his voters; it did the opposite. Americans have always favoured 'small government' and Trump promised in his 2016 campaign to reduce it further by 'draining the swamp'.

After he lost the 2020 election to Joe Biden, he attempted to overturn the result, claiming voter fraud had stolen his election. He rallied his supporters to storm the Capitol Building in January 2021. Many were subsequently arrested and charged. One of his first actions when he won the 2024 election was to pardon them all.

Since taking office in January 2025, he has surrounded himself with a cabinet of similarly politically inexperienced people, who, like him, look upon the USA, not as a country with citizens, but as a company from which they obtain dividends and manipulate as necessary for their own ends.

In this term, Trump seems to favour governing by Executive Order. One of his first was the implementation of severe trade tariffs on the rest of the world, which caused wide spread panic in financial centres. He eventually back peddled and delayed the implementation, but now Congress is questioning its legality. One hopes that the traditional checks and balances of the US political system kicks in, and Trump's authoritarian tendencies don't take root.

Trump craves a Nobel Peace Prize. Four Presidents have won the Peace Prize, including most recently Barak Obama; his nemesis. He has his sights on Ukraine; he said he'd end that war in a week and for Gaza; he suggested getting all Palestinians to leave so he could build a Dubai style resort on the Strip. He doesn't care about the process or the work it would require, he just wants the accolade. In actual fact, his actions since his election have done nothing for the cause of peace.

Abuse of power

In 2023, 4 criminal indictments were filed against Trump. These indictments, or any resulting conviction, bizarrely, would not have disqualified him from standing as a candidate in the 2024 Presidential election.

Firstly, the New York Supreme Court charged him with 34 felony counts of falsifying business records to conceal payments made to the model Stormy Daniels, hush money to buy her silence after a sexual encounter between them. He instructed his then lawyer, Michael Cohen to pay her, which he subsequently billed back to Trump as legal expenses.

This indictment was the first of a former President; he also became the first US President to be held in contempt of court over comments he made about individuals involved in the trial.

The Court for the Southern District of Florida bought a case against him for the mishandling of State documents, when many classified as 'Top Secret' were found at this home in Mar-a-Largo.

The Court for the District of Columbia charged him with attempting to overturn the 2020 Presidential election, leading to the attack on the Capitol building by Trump followers.

The Fulton County Supreme Court in Georgia, charged him with allegedly attempting to overturn Joe Biden's victory in that state. This case is still pending. The other three were dismissed.

The jurisdiction of the courts against a sitting President is now under scrutiny.

We can take from this that President Trump, leader of the free world, cares little for honesty, integrity, and truth. And even though the Constitution limits Presidents to two terms, he has said he intends to serve a third term.

Chapter 5

Vladimir Putin

Vladimir Putin was born in 1952 in St Petersburg and is 6 years younger than Donald Trump. His father had been invalided out of the army ten years earlier and there remains some controversy as to who his real mother was. At school, the young Putin would read Karl Marx, Engels, and Lenin. He took up Judo and Sambo, a particular form of Russian martial art when he was 12. Later, he would attend St Petersburg High School with a German language immersion programme. He became fluent in German and often gives speeches in that language. He studied law at the Leningrad State University and graduated in 1975. Soon after he joined the KGB

He spent 10 years of training with the KGB, before moving to Dresden with his wife, using a cover identity as a translator. He resigned from the KGB in 1991 after the fall of the Soviet Union, having reached the rank of Lieutenant Colonel, to pursue a political career.

He was active in the St Petersburg administration and the St Petersburg Mayors office until 1996, when he was called to Moscow where he became involved in managing the transfer of former Soviet assets to the Russian Federation.

In 1998, Boris Yeltsin put him in charge of the FSB, Russia's primary intelligence and security agency.

In 1999, he became acting Prime Minister, endorsed by Boris Yeltsin as his preferred successor and was elected President in 2000.

Putin has been either Prime minister or President of Russia ever since; being elected to his fourth Presidential term in 2018.

In 2014, Russia annexed Crimea and in 2022, invaded Ukraine. Just before the invasion, Putin had amassed troops along the border; perhaps in retaliation for what he saw as the inexorable creep eastwards of NATO. Whether he actually intended to invade or was just doing a bit of sabre rattling to make a point, we'll never know. That war is still ongoing, and Putin is regarded by the West as the epitome of a mad Bond villain; out to conquer all of Europe and probably the rest of the world while he's at it, and needs to be stopped at all costs.

But for all his failings as a leader, his focus is entirely on Russia, his country, instead of the naked self-interest that our other two leaders show.

.

Abuse of power

Putin put forward constitutional amendments allowing him to run for re-election twice more; potentially extending his presidency to 2036.

Under Putin's rule Russia has become an authoritarian dictatorship, and Putin tends to kill those who oppose him.

In 2002, Chechen rebels held 912 hostages in a Moscow theatre and Putin sent in special forces who released Fentanyl gas that killed the rebels and 100 of the hostages.

Putin has vocal domestic opponents in Russia; for example Boris Nemtsov accused Putin of corruption including profiteering from the Sochi Winter Olympics and wrote a number of in-depth exposes of corruption and embezzlement. He was assassinated in 2015 with his Ukrainian partner in Moscow.

Alexi Nevalny led the opposition to Putin and in 2011 founded the Anti-Corruption Foundation. In 2020 he was hospitalised and found to have been poisoned by the nerve agent,Novichok. He went to Germany for treatment but was arrested on return to Russia for breaking parole conditions;

this initial sentence was twice extended on what Amnesty International described as spurious grounds. In 2024 the Prison Service reported him dead. And Putin's reach extends to his dissenters who have left Russia. Alexander Litvinenko and Sergei Skripal were ex members of the Russian Secret services and considered traitors, capable of sharing Russian State secrets with Western powers.

Litvinenko accused Putin of ordering the assassination of Boris Berezovsky. He was arrested a year later but acquitted. He left Russia in 2000 and went to London, where the British secret services quickly enrolled him. Six years later he died of radiation poisoning from Polonium 210, after meeting two ex KGB officers who likely put it into his tea. He is buried in Highgate Cemetery in London.

Skripal was a double agent ostensibly working for the Russians while feeding information to British intelligence. He was caught and arrested for treason in 2004 but in view of his dual citizenship was part of a prisoner exchange with the UK in 2013. In 2018, he and his daughter who was visiting him from Moscow, were found poisoned by Novichok in Salisbury, but both recovered. On 7 June 2020, *The Sunday Times* reported both father and daughter alive and well at an undisclosed location in New Zealand.

Chapter 6

Benjamin Netanyahu

Netanyahu is the most articulate and educated of the leaders in this essay. He was born in Tel Aviv in October 1949, but when he was 7 the family moved to America – to Pennsylvania

In 1967, he went back to Israel to do his military service with the IDF, joined an elite commando unit and was honourably discharged in 1972. He then returned to the US to continue his education. He won a place at MIT to study architecture and received a master's degree. He went on to do a doctorate at Harvard in Political Science.

He joined the Boston Consulting Group in 1976 and in 1978, returned to Israel to set up the Yonatan Netanyahu Anti-Terrorism Institute after losing his brother Yonatan in the successful raid on Entebbe in 1976, after an Air France flight was hijacked there by the PLO. All the hostages were freed, and Yonatan Netanyahu was the only Israeli casualty.

Between 1984 and 1988, Netanyahu was the Israeli Ambassador to the UN.

In 1993, he became leader of the Opposition for the Likud party and in 1996 was elected as Israel's youngest Prime Minister. After a vote of no confidence, he was defeated in the 1999 election and resigned from politics.

He returned, as minister for foreign affairs and finance, before resigning again over the Gaza Disengagement Plan in 2005, which saw all 21 Israeli settlements in the Gaza Strip dismantled.

Netanyahu then rejoined Likud and served again as Opposition leader until the 2009 election, when he formed a coalition with other right-wing parties and was again Prime Minister. He most recently won the 2022 election, again in coalition with extreme right-wing parties. He has been the longest serving Prime Minister Israel has ever had, serving a total of 17 years.

Netanyahu, a friend of Donald Trump since the '80s, made much of the friendship when he was elected in 2016. Trump recognised Jerusalem as the capital of Israel, Israeli sovereignty over the Golan Heights and brokered the Abrahamic Accords; all to Netanyahu's advantage.

Any discussion of Israel and its current Prime Minister is largely dominated by the Palestinian/ Israeli conflict which has been ongoing ever since the formation of the State of Israel in 1948.

Most recently, on 7 October 2023, Hamas militants made a surprise attack breaching the barrier and crossed from Gaza into Southern Israel. They killed over 1,000 people at a music festival and took more than 200 hostages back into Gaza.

Israel retaliated with a full-scale war on Gaza that is ongoing as of writing. Gaza has been raised to the ground and more than 50,000 Palestinians, mostly civilian women and children, have died.

Aid deliveries immediately stopped, and Gaza was under siege. Now, after nearly 2 years of conflict, famine is widespread, as food aid is still denied. What started out as justified self-defence very quickly turned in to revenge and now, many agree, ethnic cleansing and genocide.

Netanyahu relies on the support of his extremist right wing Cabinet including Ben Gvir and Smotrich. They want Palestinians eliminated from Gaza and support settler violence against Palestinians in the West Bank. Whether Netanyahu entirely shares their right-wing views, we don't know (although we know he is not in favour of a Two State Solution), but if he wants to keep his job, he certainly needs to keep them happy.

Netanyahu regards any negative comment or criticism of his actions in Gaza as manifestations of anti-Semitism, which may be why the West has taken nearly two years to wake up and start to object to it.

Abuse of Power

Netanyahu has been criticised for security failures that led to the 7 October attack. Tensions between Israel and Hamas had been escalating by Sept 2023, and only days before, Egypt said it had warned Israel "an explosion of the situation [was] coming, and very soon, and it would be big". Israel denied receiving such a warning. Michael McCaul, Chairman of the US House Foreign Relations Committee, also said that warnings were given three days before, and Shin Bet, the internal security agency claims to have warned the government, but were ignored.

Netanyahu has long been opposed to a Two State Solution to the conflict, and some say he may have intentionally allowed the lapse in security, allowing Israel to once and for all destroy Gaza, force the Palestinian population to flee, and finally take the territory into Greater Israel.

Netanyahu's government has been accused of genocide in Gaza, culminating in the *South Africa v Israel* case before the International Court of Justice in December 2023.

The International Criminal Court issued an arrest warrant in November 2024 for Netanyahu along with former defence minister Yoav Gallant and Hamas militant Mohammed Deif, for alleged war crimes and crimes against humanity as part of the ICC Investigation in Palestine.

There are also three major indictments against Netanyahu being pursued in the courts since 2019 and awaiting the defence of each.

Over the years he and his wife received lucrative gifts from two friendly benefactors, for personal gain, colluding with and bribing a newspaper editor against another to ensure favourable political coverage in the press and accepting bribes from a major Israeli telecommunications company, abusing his position as Minister of Communications.

By summer of 2024 Israeli prosecutors had completed presenting all three cases, leaving it to Netanyahu to present his rebuttal.

He began his defence in early 2025 and juggles his position as Prime Minister with his part-time appearances in court.

In conclusion

When their fledgling new Republic was formed in the eighteenth century, the old, staid uncles in Europe and beyond may have looked upon the USA with mild disdain, as with a precocious toddler. But the toddler was to grow up to be a parent, a guardian and protector, a policeman of the world, one of two super powers whose leaders knew that with power came responsibility.

Now, though, with Donald Trump, especially in his second term, America has regressed into a stroppy teenager, refusing to come out of his room and play with the other kids and wanting instead to eat hamburgers and play computer games. Trump has abdicated himself from involvement with NATO, the UN, and many aid organisations that the US previously funded, in an isolationist, America First, to hell with the rest of the world, rant.

Trump is self-serving and craves and demands personal respect, whereas Putin only craves respect for his country. Netanyahu seems only to crave power and revenge. Edmund Burke may have implied that Great Nations require *great* minds. Undoubtedly, the USA and Russia are great nations with The State of Israel as a Middle East satellite of a great nation. And although none of our leaders could be described as a great mind, at least Putin could be said to be a grown up and possibly, given the chance, a safe pair of hands. And perhaps that's as much as we can hope for.

Donald Trump thus far, is the opposite of a safe pair of hands.

And Benjamin Netanyahu is emboldened by unwavering American support for anything he decides to do; bombing Lebanon, bombing Iran, bombing Syria, and his actions in Gaza... he seems set on destroying the entire Islamic Middle East to make Israel feel safe. Of course, the instability caused by such a course of action will reverberate around the region and the rest of the world, resulting in no one feeling safe, least of all the State of Israel.

Chapter 7

The Future

A Prayer for now and the future

May we be truthful, authentic and compassionate.

May we seek peace, where there is conflict.

And love where there is hatred and division.

– Anonymous.

Gaza and Middle East

The full credit to this seed of an idea comes from Shlomo Sand, the Emeritus Professor of History at Tel Aviv University. For years he supported the idea of a Two State Solution with the independence of a Palestinian state. After the 7 October attack, however, he discussed whether there was a more realistic and achievable solution. His second book, Israel – Palestine: Federation or Apartheid, is written with scholarship, erudition and a wealth of historical background. I hope he can forgive me, in expressing a very simple picture of how such a structure might play out in the future.

To that end, I ask for your indulgence in the following fantasy:

Having had more than 150 years of warfare, bloodshed, broken accords and lives tormented by fear, a new country was created in 2035 (*feel free to put your own dates here*), called New Jerusalem. Citizens of New Jerusalem were all of equal status under the law, be they of Jewish, Islamic or Christian origin.

The Capital of New Jerusalem is the old town of Jerusalem, now a thriving international city housing the Federal Parliament. Major hotels have sprung up as well as one of the newest and largest airports in the Middle East.

The Federation comprises four main regions: Jerusalem, Israel, Gaza, and the West Bank. The regional capitals were, apart from Jerusalem, Tel Aviv, Gaza City, and Hebron. Citizens of New Jerusalem were free to travel, work and live anywhere in the country and strict anti- discriminatory laws were enforced.

Following the cessation of fighting and the agreement to the creation of the Federation, work began in earnest on the reconstruction of the country primarily in the Gaza region. This reconstruction was funded by many countries including the United States, Saudi Arabia, Egypt, Jordan, Israel, and Europe.

Today New Jerusalem is one of the most popular holiday destinations and business centres.

Why Not?

Crimea and The Donbas

In 2030 or thereabouts Russia and Ukraine reach an accord to end all warfare between them.

Russia agrees to lease Crimea, the Donbas and all access routes to Crimea from Ukraine for 50 to100 years. In the accord, Russia accepts the sovereignty of Ukraine albeit not any historical sovereignty.

There will be discussions opened on the reunification of the Eastern Orthodox Church as any schism between them on political rather than religious grounds will be removed.

The accord also agrees that Ukraine shall not become part of NATO and that any policing of the Accord will be overseen directly by a subcommittee of the Security Council of The United Nations.

All financial sanctions against Russia will be removed and Russia will compensate and be allowed to work in Ukraine on the reconstruction and rebuilding of damaged and destroyed properties.

All prisoners of war will be freed by both sides. However, both education and language will be determined on a regional basis.

There will be free access to live and work in any part of Ukraine by all its citizens although the Russian language will be the first language of Crimea and the West. Neither party will be allowed any long-range weapons or foreign militia and intelligence support.

Why Not?

Trump and the USA

This section was one of most difficult due to the unpredictability of Donald Trump and his erratic and highly volatile actions. We cannot exclude that those characteristics themselves might result in his losing power during the next four years either by his resignation or perhapsby his assassination.

A UK phone in programme was even suggesting that America might become effectively a Fascist State with Trump imprisoning dissenters, abandoning all semblance of government oversight, surrounding himself with fanatically loyal lieutenants and remaining in power until he decides to relinquish control.

However, I do believe in the strength of the US constitution, although maybe with some new amendments. Perhaps the Electoral College system of voting has, after 200 years outlived its usefulness? As indeed, the right to bear arms? In 4 years, Trump will be democratically gone, albeit with some short-lived shenanigans on his part, no doubt, and the USA will return to its rightful position as the leader and defender of the Free World.

Before this happens, though, the Democratic Party needs to seek out and promote a charismatic and telegenic leader with great communication skills of the ilk of John F Kennedy and Barack Obama. These individuals exist and someone is waiting and able to take on this mantle. Of course, such a fair-minded and democratic individual might also be found within the Republican Party.

Why Not? Just find him or her soon.

Further Reading

USA

- The Penguin History of the USA — Hugh Brogan
- Too Much and Never Enough — Mary L. Trump
- The House of Trump: The House of Putin — Craig Unger

Israel

- The Invention of the Jewish People — Shlomo Sand
- Israel -Palestine: Federation or Apartheid — Shlomo Sand
- The Resistible Rise of Benjamin Netanyahu — Neill Lochery

Russia

- We Need to Talk About Putin — Mark Galeotti
- First Person — Vladimir Putin
- Putin's People — Catherine Belton
- Karl Marx — Francis Wheen